For Julia & family
Thank you for your endless support!
Have a peaceful and healthy Christmas!
Love, Jane ♡

To my parents,
who made my whole childhood
magical, not only at Christmas.
Thank you for your endless
love and support.
I love you.

QUINN SAVES CHRISTMAS

Copyright©2020 by Jana Buchmann

All rights reserved. No parts of this publication, or the characters in it, may be reproduced or distributed in any form or by any means without prior written consent from the publisher.
For copyright permissions, school visits, and book readings/signings please email

janabuchmannauthor@gmail.com.

Written by Jana Buchmann
Illustrated by Lara Korotenko
ISBN Paperback 978-1-7354586-5-6
ISBN Hardcover 978-1-7354586-7-0
ISBN Ebook 978-1-7354586-6-3
Library of Congress Control Number: 2020921142

First edition 2020
Printed in the USA
www.janabuchmann.com

QUINN SHINYFROST is a curious snow fairy who LOVES adventures! She also LOVES storytime at her fairy school. She ESPECIALLY LOVES the stories about the dangerous icy blue mountains. She wonders if they are true.

One day, QUINN is DANCING and SWIRLING through the magic forest when she hears a voice.

"Nooooo! I'm sure I gave it to you! Santa needs the list! Where did you put it?"

Quinn Loves Christmas!

"*I wonder what happened to Santa's list?*" she asks herself. ***"I'm ready to find out!"***

She leans forward to hear better.

A little bit more...

        A little bit more.

"Whoops! Sorry!" she says. "I heard you arguing. What happened? Do you need help?"

One of the elves takes a DEEP BREATH.

"Santa asked us to pick up his wish list and start making toys. I know I gave it to Rusty, but it's gone!"

"You had it, Fudge! You kept it when we left Santa's house!" Rusty shouts.

"Stop arguing!" QUINN says.

"You probably lost the list on the way to your workshop. Let's follow your tracks back and see if we can find it."

They follow the elves' tracks through the
MAGIC FOREST, their shoes SQUEAKING in the snow.

Then...
What is that?

"This looks like a piece of Santa's list!" Rusty says.
"I wonder who has such big feet," QUINN tells the elves.

"I'm ready to find out!"

The **GIGANTIC FOOTPRINTS** lead to the end of the forest and toward the **ICY BLUE MOUNTAINS.**

QUINN hesitates.

Should they follow them further?
Are the SCARY STORIES she has heard at storytime true?
Quinn takes a deep breath and straightens her shoulders.

"I'm ready to find out!"

Together, QUINN and the elves march up the mountain until they reach the top. QUINN can't believe her eyes!

"It's the biggest and most beautiful icy house I've ever seen!" she says.

"Whoever lives here can't be so bad! **I'm ready to find out!**"

"*Quinn! Listen!*" whispers Rusty.

There is a strange HOWLING NOISE.

"*Someone is crying!*" says QUINN. She heads toward the giant door. "Hello? Anyone home?"

The sobbing stops.

There is a RUMBLE followed by the sound of HEAVY steps.

The door opens.

"Hello? What do you want?" the HAIRY CREATURE asks.

"Quinn!" Fudge points to the creature's hand and whispers, "That looks like the piece of paper we found near the footprints!"

"Mister...Yeti," QUINN says, as she read the name 'Yeti' on the mailbox, "It seems that you have stolen Santa's list!"

"Whoooohoooohooo!" Yeti sobs.
"I didn't know it was Santa's list!"

"Why did you take it in the first place?" QUINN asks.

"I needed something to protect my bird feeder from the snow, and it looked perfect,"

YETI explains. "But when I realized it was Santa's list, I felt so bad. I don't want to ruin Christmas for all the children!"

"Why didn't you walk to the workshop and give it back?" QUINN asks.

"Because I don't know how to find it," answers YETI.

"I never leave the icy blue mountains except when I go skating at the moon lake. I found the list on my way back to my house last night."

"You must be very lonely," says QUINN.
"Don't you want to have friends?" she asks.

"I've never had a friend. I don't know how friendship works,"

YETI answers quietly. "I once had a pen friend, but the postman was too scared to come up again because of my signs."

"Well, friends help each other. That's what they're for," QUINN says. She looks at Rusty and Fudge, who nod in agreement. "Let's protect your bird feeder together," says QUINN. "I already have an idea."

"Thank you so much! I'm so happy you ignored my signs and came up to my house!" YETI beams.

"Do you mind taking Santa's list back to his workshop for me? I have a lot of work to do. I need to remove my signs."

"Aren't you worried more strangers will come to visit you?" QUINN asks.

"I'm ready to find out!" YETI responds with a grin.

Jana Buchmann

Jana Buchmann is a children's book author and mom of three girls with a love of storytelling. She enjoys combining unique ideas with magic and imagination to create memorable stories that bring tons of fun and smiles to every child who reads them.

When not writing, Jana enjoys reading, traveling, being creative, and spending time with her daughters. She also volunteers for an organization that reads and streams children's books for kids in a hospital.

Visit www.janabuchmann.com for free activity booklets, fun blog posts about books and crafts, and creative ideas to spark your child's imagination. Sign up for Jana's newsletter to be the first to know about new titles, more coming soon!

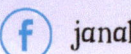 janabuchmannauthor   janabuchmann_author

Check out Jana's other titles! More coming soon!

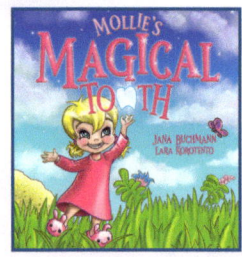 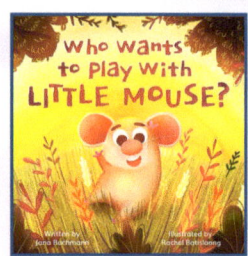

Lara Korotenko

Lara Korotenko is a talented Ukrainian artist from Kiev. She discovered her love and passion for art as young as 5, when she hosted a local children's TV show about drawing. Since then, Lara has been very busy: she has illustrated children's pages for newspapers, books, magazines, advertisements and games and she makes stunning oil paintings, too. But most of all, she just loves to draw children's book illustrations!

Lara's motto in life is "a creative person's inner child never grows up".

 www.artstation.com/lorri   korotenkolorri/

Quinn's Snowflake Cookies

Ingredients

1 cup (2 sticks) butter, soft   1 teaspoon vanilla extract
½ cup powdered sugar   2¼ cups all purpose flour
+ 1 cup powdered sugar for coating

Directions

1. Preheat oven to 400 degrees F.
2. Using a large mixing bowl, mix butter and powdered sugar together. Add in vanilla extract.
3. Add flour and mix until soft dough ball forms.
4. Roll dough into 1 inch balls and place on an ungreased cookie sheet.
5. Bake for 8-10 minutes or until cookies are set but not browning.
6. Remove from oven, let cool for a few minutes then roll in a bowl of powdered sugar.
7. Place on cooling rack to cool, then roll in powdered sugar again.

Enjoy!

CPSIA information can be obtained
at www.ICGtesting.com
Printed in the USA
BVHW021541191220
595970BV00002B/15

Dedicated in Loving Memory of
Henry J. Callis
The man who taught me to dream.